bubblefacts...

BRITISH HISTORY

Miles KeLLy

PUBLISHING

First published in 2006 by
Miles Kelly Publishing Ltd
Bardfield Centre, Great Bardfield, Essex, CM7 4SL

Copyright © Miles Kelly Publishing Ltd 2006

2 4 6 8 10 9 7 5 3 1

Publishing Director:
Anne Marshall

Senior Editor:
Belinda Gallagher

Designer:
Louisa Leitao

Cartoons:
Mark Davis

Production:
Elizabeth Brunwin

ISBN 1-84236-655-6

Reprographics: Mike Coupe, Ian Paulyn

Printed in China

British Library Cataloguing-in-Publication Data
A catalogue record for this book is available from the British Library

Indexer: Jane Parker

www.mileskelly.net
info@mileskelly.net

Contents

Stone and bronze
making tools

Human beings first lived in Great Britain about 37,000 years ago. By 6000BC, hunters in Britain had become skilled at making tools such as needles, fish hooks and harpoons. They hunted deer, boar and wild oxen in the oak forests. Animal skins were used to make clothes and they also provided coverings for shelters.

Flint was an excellent stone to make tools with. These razor-sharp tools were used to hunt animals.

Some of the Stonehenge pillars were as heavy as 20 elephants. They were hauled from 215 kilometres away.

Massive pillars of stone were used to create Stonehenge. The stones were positioned so that they lined up with the rising and setting Sun. It is thought that Stonehenge was used to observe the Sun, Moon and stars. People would have crowded into the circle on midsummer morning to watch the rising of the Sun.

DON'T LIKE THE LOOK OF THAT SOUP.

PUT SOME EFFORT INTO IT!

SIZZLE!

PERSONAL PORTRAITS FOR FREE!

Hot, liquid bronze was later used to make metal tools. Stonehenge was built between 3000 and 1500BC.

Celtic capers

warriors and forts

Around 600BC, warriors from mainland Europe began to settle in parts of the British Isles. Many of them belonged to a group of people called the Celts. Those people already living in the British Isles slowly adopted the Celtic way of life. They began to speak Celtic languages, too.

Many British Celts lived in villages of large round houses. Most Celts were farmers or blacksmiths.

The Celts were first-rate metal workers. They realized that iron was a hard, useful metal. In fact, people who had not seen iron before thought that it had magical properties. Some people still nail iron horseshoes onto doors for good luck.

The safest place to be when war broke out was on top of a hill! These places were easily defended with ditches and wooden fences.

The Celts were show-offs and liked to look good! Chariots and swords were used in times of battle.

Ruled by Rome

invaded!

The Romans first came to Britain in 55BC. However, it was not until AD43 that they conquered most of the land. Only the north of Scotland remained free of Roman rule. In AD122, the Romans built Hadrian's Wall. This marked the northern border of an empire that stretched from Spain, to North Africa, and the Black Sea.

In AD60, Queen Boudicca rebelled against the Romans. She burned down towns, but was eventually defeated.

The Romans liked their comforts. Rich people lived in luxurious country houses called villas. These even had under-floor central heating.

Roman soldiers began to leave Britain in AD401. Many parts of the Roman empire were under attack. In Britain there were rebellions. Pirates sailed the seas. The Irish attacked western shores. The city of Rome itself was captured by German warriors in AD476.

The Romans opened public baths where people could have a hot or cold dip. Long, straight roads were built.

Under attack!
Anglo-Saxons

People from Germany began to attack eastern Britain. More and more of them landed in the 400s and 500s. They belonged to various peoples known as Angles, Saxons, Jutes and Frisians. We call them Anglo-Saxons. Their speech became the English language, mixed with Celtic and Latin.

OUT OF TUNE...

LAND OF MILK AND HONEY.

LAND OF SHEEP!

BAA BAA!

The Anglo-Saxons slowly conquered the south and east of Britain. They divided it into separate kingdoms.

The first Christians in Britain were Romans. The Anglo-Saxons still worshipped their own gods.

King Alfred ruled the kingdom of Wessex from 871 to 899. His army fought off Danish invaders.

Viking raiders

Britain attacked

The Vikings were pirates, raiders, explorers, traders and farmers. Some people called them Northmen, or Danes, as their homeland was Norway, Sweden and Denmark. Viking raiders began to attack the British Isles in 789. They were soon feared far and wide.

Viking longships carried warriors inland to towns and villages where they could steal treasure.

The Vikings fought against the Anglo-Saxons and soon controlled large areas of England. In 1016, England even had a Viking king, Cnut I. Vikings also ruled the Isle of Man and large areas of Scotland and Ireland.

Can you believe it?

Before they went into battle, Viking warriors (berserkirs) worked themselves up into a frenzy. This is where the word 'berserk' comes from.

The Vikings stole livestock and made people slaves. They realized that Britain provided good farmland.

Norman conquerors

France attacks

William, Duke of Normandy, was descended from the Vikings. Although William was French, he thought he had a claim to the English throne. In 1066 William crossed the Channel with a fleet of ships. His aim was to become king of England.

William's army met the English in a great battle near Hastings in Sussex.

The Normans created the Domesday Book. In it they recorded the houses and lands in their new kingdom. People had to work for their new Norman lords, and pay taxes. The Domesday Book helped the king to keep track of everything.

English King Harold was killed, and the Normans marched to London. William was crowned king of England.

Knights and castles

riding into battle

The Normans began to build castles in Britain. The first castles were made of wood, but before long they were made with thick stone walls and towers. Water-filled ditches called moats surrounded them. Castles were built in Britain for the next 400 years.

The most important soldiers were knights. They practised fighting in mock battles called tournaments

Can you believe it?

A knight's armour weighed around 13 kilograms. Add to that the weight of all the weapons – and pity the poor horse!

Each noble family had its own badge called a coat-of-arms. This appeared on shields and flags and helped to show which knight was which during a battle. There were strict rules about the design of coats-of-arms, known as heraldry.

Banquets were held in the great hall of a castle. Venison (deer), swan and goose were often served.

Middle Ages

town life

Towns were still small in the Middle Ages, and surrounded by high walls. Streets were narrow, muddy, and smelly, too. Houses and buildings were built from timber, which meant they could catch fire easily.

A market was usually held once a week. During the Middle Ages, many towns were protected by a castle.

Few people could read. Special signs were hung outside shops so that people knew what was being sold. This sign shows that pottery, such as jugs, bowls and pots, is for sale.

Knights and squires on their way to tournaments would stop off in towns to buy food and drink.

Tudor times...
...Stewart, too!

The Tudors ruled England and Wales after 1485. They also controlled a small part of Ireland, around Dublin. The Tudor rulers and nobles liked to live in fine palaces rather than draughty castles. The Stewart family ruled Scotland. Their greatest king was James IV. He was killed in battle in 1513.

The first Tudor king, Henry VII, united England under his rule. James IV built a fine fleet of ships.

Henry VIII became king of England in 1509. He married six times. Two of his wives were beheaded.

During the 1500s people argued about religion. Mary I ordered people to be burned at the stake.

Good Queen Bess!
last of the Tudors

Elizabeth I was the daughter of Henry VIII. She became queen in 1558 and she had her father's temper, as well as his love of music, dancing and fine clothes. Unlike her father, Elizabeth never married. She was also a much wiser ruler than Henry. The last of the Tudors, Elizabeth died in 1603.

BIT TOO MUCH MEAD!

A NICE LAMB KEBAB WITH CHILI SAUCE...

AT YOUR SERVICE, MA'AM.

LAMB? BLEAT!

During Elizabeth's reign, Francis Drake sailed right around the world. Elizabeth made him a knight.

Parts of England grew wealthy as merchants sold cloth across Europe. Mary Queen of Scots was executed.

In the 1590s, theatres grew popular. People crowded into them to see the plays of William Shakespeare.

Plots and plans

fireworks!

After Elizabeth I died, the throne passed to James VI of Scotland. James was the son of Mary Queen of Scots. He now also became James I of England. James proved to be an intelligent king who wrote about the dangers of tobacco and introduced a new English translation of the Bible. He was succeeded by his son, Charles I.

In 1605, Guy Fawkes was accused of plotting to blow up the Houses of Parliament. Charles I started a civil w

oliver cromwell was more famous as a football player than as a politician. football didn't have many rules in those days!

Charles I started the Civil War in 1642. He quarrelled with Parliament about religion and taxes. This lead to six years of fighting. Eventually, Charles was put on trial and beheaded. For 11 years, England had no king. At first a Council of State ran the country. Then in 1653 Parliament chose the commander of the Roundheads, Oliver Cromwell, to rule as Lord Protector.

ROUNDHEAD, YOU'RE DEAD!

THAT'S A CAVALIER ATTITUDE!

DON'T LIKE THIS GAME ANYMORE...

TOO BAD!

The king's soldiers were Cavaliers and the soldiers of Parliament were Roundheads. The Roundheads won.

Plague and fire

dangerous times

In 1665 the plague, or Black Death, returned to London. Thousands of people died. The disease was spread by rat fleas, but people didn't know this. City folk fled to the countryside, taking their deadly germs with them. Then in 1666, a spark from a fire set a bakery alight. The Great Fire of London had started.

The Great Fire raged throughout London for five days. Much of the city had to be rebuilt in stone.

When Charles II died in 1665, his brother became James II of England. However James was a Catholic, and the Protestant supporters threw him off the throne. James' daughter became Queen Mary II, ruling jointly with her Protestant husband, William III.

Can you believe it?

The first cannons did more harm to the soldiers firing them than to the enemy! In 1460, an exploding cannon killed James II of Scotland.

OUT WITH THE OLD!

BUT I'M THE KING!

STAND AND DELIVER!

WHAT? PAPERS? SPEECHES?

James II was thrown off the throne in 1688. During the 1600s and 1700s, highwaymen held up coaches.

Wealthy and powerful
Industrial Age

Queen Victoria ruled from 1837 to 1901. During this time, Britain became wealthy and powerful. It was the Industrial Age, and Britain's empire also expanded. However, many people were still desperately poor. They worked in factories, mills and coal mines. Pay was low and work was dangerous.

Queen Victoria also became Empress of India. Many people were so poor they had little or no money.

can you believe it?

Bathing in the sea became popular in Victorian times. People changed in bathing machines, which were then hauled into the sea!

Cities and factories spread across the Scottish Lowlands, the north of England, the Midlands, South Wales and Northern Ireland. Factories used cotton, rubber and timber from other areas of the empire and produced goods that were shipped around the world.

YOU NEED A GOOD BATH!

IT'S LOUIS VUITTON LUGGAGE, YOU KNOW!

DROPPED MY CONTACT LENS...

SQUAWK!

...me people moved to different areas of the empire, which included parts of Africa, Asia and the Americas.

Modern times

world wars

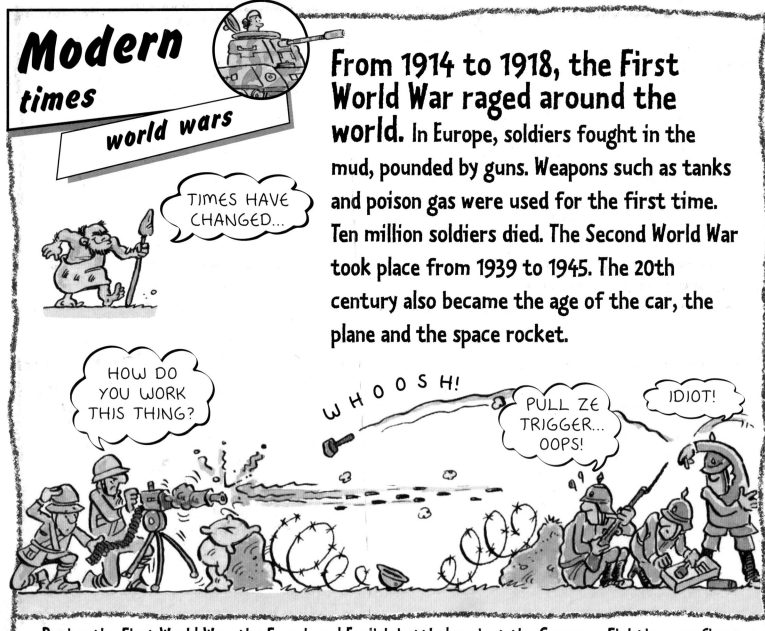

From 1914 to 1918, the First World War raged around the world. In Europe, soldiers fought in the mud, pounded by guns. Weapons such as tanks and poison gas were used for the first time. Ten million soldiers died. The Second World War took place from 1939 to 1945. The 20th century also became the age of the car, the plane and the space rocket.

During the First World War, the French and English battled against the Germans. Fighting was fierce.

In 1918, women over 30 were given the right to vote. The Second World War was the worst war in history.

Millions of people died during both World Wars. Inventions changed everyone's lives in the 20th century.

Index